D1472546

COPING WHEN

A PARENT
HAS PTSD

Mary-Lane Kamberg

Rosen
YA
™

MASTICS MORICHES SHIRLEY
New York

For Rebekah

Published in 2018 by The Rosen Publishing Group, Inc.
29 East 21st Street, New York, NY 10010

Library of Congress Cataloging-in-Publication Data

Names: Kamberg, Mary-Lane, 1948– author.
Title: Coping when a parent has PTSD / Mary-Lane Kamberg.
Other titles: Coping when a parent has post-traumatic stress disorder
Description: First edition. | New York, NY : Rosen Publishing, 2018. |
  Series: Coping | Audience: Grades 7–12. | Includes bibliographical
  references and index.
Identifiers: LCCN 2016056439 | ISBN 9781508173861 (library bound)
Subjects: LCSH: Post-traumatic stress disorder. | Post-traumatic stress
  disorder—Patients—Family relationships.
Classification: LCC RC552.P67 K355 2018 | DDC 616.85/21—dc23
LC record available at https://lccn.loc.gov/2016056439

Manufactured in the United States of America

CONTENTS

Kendall stood at the airport gate waiting for her dad to arrive home from combat in the Middle East. She held a small American flag on a wooden stick. So did her mom and her two younger brothers. Her mom also held the family golden retriever's leash. The dog wore a blue bandanna with white stars around his neck.

Kendall was first to spot her father. "There he is!" she shouted. She waved her flag. The rest of the family cheered and waved their flags, too. The joyous welcome included hugs and kisses all around. Kendall had missed her father so much while he was away, but she knew they'd make up for lost time now that he was home.

The family's happiness was short lived. Although the soldier said

Post-traumatic stress disorder, or PTSD, affects not only the person who has it. It also affects family members, including those of service members.

4

he was glad to be home, his actions didn't show it. He seemed jumpy all the time. Noise bothered him—even the sounds his children made when they were playing games on the kitchen table. He withdrew from them and spent most of his time sitting in an easy chair in the living room. Some nights Kendall heard him crying out from nightmares.

Before her father left on his deployment, he and Kendall had always been close. Now that he was back, she tried to reach out to him, but he shrugged her away. The worst was the night she starred in her high school's production of the musical *Les Misérables*. Her father was too tired to come watch her perform. She thought he didn't love her any more. What had she done wrong? At the same time, she was worried about him. She didn't know what to do.

Kendall's father was showing signs of post-traumatic stress disorder, commonly called PTSD. The disorder is a lasting result of experiencing a traumatic event. PTSD is commonly associated with trauma experienced during war. However, it also occurs in victims of crime or assault and those involved in natural disasters, serious accidents, or other threatening situations. According to *Psychology Today*, trauma is "anything that is too much, too soon, or too fast for our nervous system to handle, especially if we can't reach a successful resolution."

As Kendall's family soon learned, PTSD affects more than the person who experienced the trauma. It affects the entire family. At first, the family focused on getting help for their soldier. Before long, however, they realized they needed help as well.

In this book, you'll learn about the causes of and treatments for PTSD and ways you can help your loved one. You'll also see the kinds of issues families face, what symptoms people with PTSD exhibit, and coping mechanisms they can use to deal with the situation. You'll also find communities of other families dealing with the same kinds of circumstances. They can support you as you deal with your own emotions and circumstances.

CHAPTER ONE

What Is PTSD?

Over the last two decades, post-traumatic stress disorder (PTSD) has often been in the news. PTSD refers to a set of symptoms arising from some kind of trauma. The PTSD Association of Canada defines trauma as an event where "serious physical harm occurred or was threatened that caused intense fear, helplessness, or horror." Another way the association explains trauma is "an unexpected event that the person cannot prepare for and can do nothing to prevent."

Examples are experiencing or witnessing military combat, terrorist attacks, natural disasters, serious accidents, or such crimes as kidnapping, rape, or other physical assaults. Lesser known, but just as potentially serious, are such events as the death of a loved one, loss of a job, divorce, domestic violence, failing to achieve a goal, or serious personal injury. Individuals experience

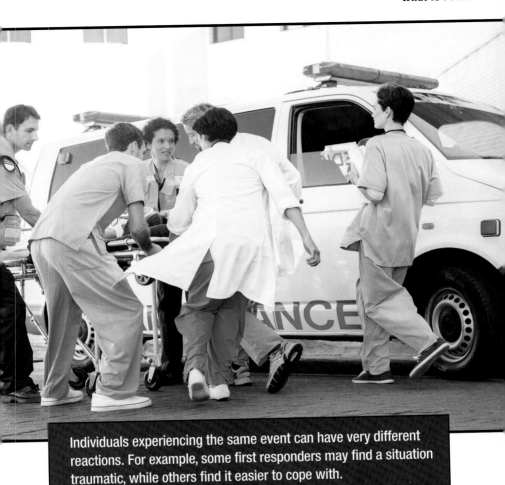

Individuals experiencing the same event can have very different reactions. For example, some first responders may find a situation traumatic, while others find it easier to cope with.

similar events differently. One person may be able to handle an experience that incapacitates another and be able to deal with the resulting emotions.

For instance, paramedics responding to gun violence may respond to the sight of a victim bleeding in the street without experiencing deep trauma. A bystander who feels weak in the knees may be highly traumatized by the same exact thing.

Some individuals feel numb during trauma. They feel nothing at all, or check out emotionally. Some experience the event in a detached state, as if it's happening to someone else. This reaction, called disassociation, can arise from repeated sexual or physical abuse. If they later experience PTSD, they may not associate it with the event that caused it, because their emotional shutdown was a coping tactic.

Be careful not to judge a parent's (or anyone's) reaction based on how you think you might have reacted to the same situation. It's important to remember that PTSD is a normal response to an ordeal. Just as everyone reacts in an individual way to a frightening event, those with PTSD have different experiences after the trauma. Your parent isn't weak or crazy. Rather, he or she may need care and patience.

Signs of Trouble

Symptoms of PTSD vary according to the individual, as well as the kind of trauma suffered. No one has all of them, but it's common to exhibit more than one emotion or behavior related to the stress the person suffered. The keys to diagnosis are symptoms that last longer than three months, cause the person great distress, or disrupt work or home life. Patients with PTSD may report one or more of the following emotions and behaviors:

- Reliving the event through memories, nightmares, or flashbacks.
- Responding to triggers that remind them of the event or make the event seem recurring.
- Avoiding thinking, talking about, or attending situations that remind them of the event.
- Staying out of crowds.
- Leaving driving to others.
- Skipping movies that have or may have scenes related to their trauma or remind them of it.
- Formerly positive or loving relationships turning sour.
- Forgetting or refusing to talk about aspects of the trauma.
- Feelings of distrust toward others.
- Feeling jittery or irritable most of the time.
- Feeling on guard against danger, even when seemingly completely safe.
- Having trouble sleeping.
- Having trouble concentrating.
- Being easily startled by loud noise or unexpected happenings.
- Keeping one's back to a wall for protection in public places.

In a Corner of the Mind

Many PTSD sufferers experience a traumatic event again and again, often in the form of unwanted memories. Sometimes, for no apparent reason, violent images or thoughts just pop into a person's mind. Or, during a relaxing period with little going on, the person will dwell on the past experience. Sometimes something similar to the event triggers unwanted memories of the real thing. If an attacker was bald, for example, and the victim sees another bald man, memories of the attacker might surface.

Memories may cause nightmares. The bad dreams may include scenes from the trauma itself. Or, they may be unrelated images that still scare or even terrify them enough to wake in a cold sweat. Falling back asleep may be difficult or impossible. The person with PTSD may eventually simply avoid going to bed.

In Distress

A reminder of trauma can trigger intense emotional or physical distress without necessarily bringing up memories of the ordeal. The distress may take the form of fear, guilt, shame, anger, or sadness, even when the person does not consciously connect the reminder with the actual trauma. Such reminders cause tension and anxiety. One reaction can be a full-blown panic attack.

Frequent insomnia, nightmares, or other sleep disturbances may be symptoms of PTSD. Other signs of the disorder include persistent thoughts and memories of the traumatic event.

A panic attack is a period of intense fear that occurs suddenly. Most commonly, a panic attack will cause chest pain and shortness of breath. Many people having panic attacks may feel like they are having heart attacks. Other signs include a fast heart rate, trembling, a burning sensation in the face or neck, flashes of heat or cold, sweating, nausea, dizziness, tingling, or feelings of choking or smothering. Panic attacks cause such severe anxiety that sufferers may fear another one and avoid situations similar to the one in which the attack occurred.

On Guard

Survivors of trauma know what being in danger is like. Afterward, they may have trouble relaxing or feeling safe even though the danger has passed. The body's protection system, which includes a flight-or-fight response, causes them to stay alert to potential threats everywhere around them. A person with PTSD who has this symptom, known as hyper-vigilance, may constantly look out for potential threats everywhere he or she goes.

Both bad memories and hyper-vigilance can make concentrating on work or other activities of daily life difficult. The strong focus on the past and staying on guard prevents the person from paying attention to such important information as work assignments or discussions with friends and family. Instead, he or she pays attention only to potential danger.

Flashbacks

Flashbacks are stronger than regular memories. A flashback is a memory so intense that the person believes the trauma actually is occurring again and is usually set off by a reminder of the event. Triggers can be as varied as looking at a photo, smelling an odor, hearing a noise, tasting a certain food, touching something, or being at a certain location.

A flashback happens when the person is awake. It may be triggered by a sound, sight, smell, taste, or texture in the environment that reminds him or her of similar stimuli from the original ordeal. A person having a flashback may think, feel, or act like the traumatic event that brought on PTSD is actually happening again. They may become disoriented and may fight, cry, scream, or run from the perceived threat. Although flashbacks are well documented, they are less common than other symptoms of PTSD.

A flashback can happen for a short period of time while the person still stays in touch with some elements of the present. Other flashbacks can be more severe and make a person think he or she is back at the scene of the trauma while losing all

(continued on the next page)

(continued from the previous page)

touch with reality. A military veteran, for example, might be shopping in a clothing store when his surroundings seem to change to look like a desert, and other shoppers seem to turn into enemy soldiers.

Some PTSD patients can tell a flashback is about to occur. Signs include a look of fuzziness in the environment, a feeling of separating from surroundings, or a feeling of losing touch with other people or themselves.

The nearly constant state of watchfulness keeps stress levels high. The stress can appear as high levels of irritability or anger caused by seemingly minor incidents. Even in the case of more severe stimulation, the irritation and anger may seem out of proportion to the event. Keep in mind that the person may have good reason to feel angry and, more importantly, be unable to control the intensity of his or her reaction. The anger can lead to fighting, striking out, or other aggressive behavior. The person may develop a fear of losing control when angry.

Just as memories can trigger nightmares that interfere with the trauma survivor's sleep, staying on guard can cause difficulty sleeping. If the person thinks he or she must stay awake to listen for sounds of an intruder or other threat, relaxing into a restful

PTSD can mean dwelling on memories of trauma. Continually thinking about the event interferes with sleep as well as the ability to relax when awake.

state—let alone sleep—may be difficult or impossible. Another cause of wakefulness is ruminating thoughts. Rumination is an obsession with repeated thoughts about a situation or event, including trauma. Again, the result is an inability to relax or fall asleep. Even trauma survivors who do get to sleep report that they don't feel rested when they wake up.

Avoiding Triggers

If someone experiences a traumatic event and then keeps returning to it in significantly unpleasant ways, avoiding situations or other triggers that bring him or her back to the ordeal is a normal response. Trauma survivors often exhibit avoidance symptoms.

For example, they try to avoid thoughts or feelings about the event. Or, they try to stay away from sensory images like smells or sounds that remind them, too. Some may stop watching televised news for fear of seeing something similar to their experience. If a family member or friend wants to talk about the ordeal, the trauma survivor may refuse to answer, change the subject, or simply leave the room.

Another form of avoidance is feeling distant or isolating oneself from others. Some survivors fear rejection if others notice signs of their distress. Many build walls between themselves and family members or friends. Another contributor to this detachment is difficulty trusting or confiding in others or thinking others won't be able to understand what the person with PTSD is going through.

Because of the emotional toll of the trauma, some survivors have trouble feeling love or happiness. Or, they lose interest in things they once enjoyed. They may also lose hope for the future or believe their lives will be cut short at any time. Some never feel safe and

Some PTSD sufferers believe they'll never feel safe or happy again. Some also feel survivor's guilt for surviving something that others didn't.

wonder if they ever will again or dwell on thoughts of death or dying.

Other effects of PTSD include feelings of guilt, sometimes called survivor's guilt. Survivor's guilt is an emotion, sometimes reported by survivors of a catastrophe, associated with thinking they've done something wrong by coming away from the event alive or having suffered less, or sustained less serious injury than others who died or suffered more.

All in the Head?

It isn't simple for a parent with PTSD (or any sufferer) to just snap out of it and move on. The symptoms you see may seem to be all in his or her head. In a way you're right, but PTSD is a whole body experience. The brain is central to it. Neuroimaging studies using magnetic resonance imaging (MRIs) and computerized tomography (CT) scans have been conducted on individuals with PTSD. These studies have demonstrated that PTSD changes the brain's structure

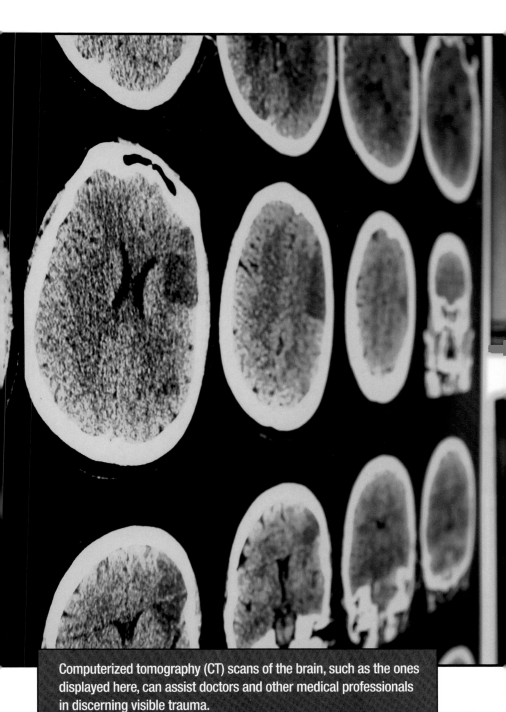

Computerized tomography (CT) scans of the brain, such as the ones displayed here, can assist doctors and other medical professionals in discerning visible trauma.

and functions, especially in areas affected by stress. Parts of the brain also trigger extreme reactions to stress when warranted. This can include the release of hormones associated with anxiety and aggression.

Three psychiatrists at the University of Michigan's Veterans Affairs Medical Center, writing in *Neuron* magazine in October 2016, reported that their research indicated that those with PTSD process memories differently from people without PTSD. Israel Liberzon, Jennifer Britton, and K. Luan Phan reported that PTSD was likely to partially result from altered physical processes in the brain. Such physical changes interfere with the person's ability to cope with stress, fear, and other emotions.

Myths & FACTS

Myth: PTSD is a sign of weakness.

Fact: PTSD is neither a sign of mental weakness nor weak character. It's a normal response to an uncommon and sometimes life-threatening experience.

Myth: People with PTSD are dangerous.

Fact: Outbursts of anger or violence are not universal symptoms of PTSD. The symptoms a person experiences and how severe they are depend on the individual.

Myth: Nothing can be done for those with PTSD.

Fact: People with PTSD cannot just get over their symptoms. However, different types of treatment have been effective for many different sufferers.

CHAPTER TWO

Who Gets PTSD?

You may wonder why your parent developed PTSD when others—even those involved in the same situation—did not. The answer is the disorder can happen to anyone. Men, women, and even children have experienced its effects. PTSD can occur at any age, with twenty being the average age of onset, according to the National Alliance on Mental Illness (NAMI).

Combat veterans and other military personnel who experienced trauma in military situations (such as sexual assault) are perhaps the best known. However, people who have been diagnosed with PTSD include victims of disaster, terrorism, sexual or physical abuse, and even car accidents. Also affected are such first responders as police officers, firefighters, emergency medical

Many people associate PTSD with military service, and combat veterans are more likely than the general population to have it. Families of service members should stay on the lookout for it.

technicians (EMTs), and doctors, nurses, and other health care workers who treat them after the events.

According to NAMI, about 8 million adults in the United States have PTSD each year, but this number is only a small part of all adults who have experienced trauma. About 60 percent of men and 50 percent of women experience trauma sometime in their lives.

Not all of them develop PTSD, but about 10 percent of women and 4 percent of men do.

Statistics are higher for members of the US military. In 2016, the US Department of Veterans Affairs estimated that PTSD occurs in about 15 percent of veterans of the war in Vietnam, 12 percent of participants in Desert Storm, and between 11 percent and 20 percent of military personnel in Operations Iraqi Freedom and Enduring Freedom.

PTSD in History

Researchers think that Florence Nightingale, the founder of modern nursing; American poet Emily Dickinson; and other historical figures suffered from PTSD long before the disorder was identified as a distinct diagnosis. Based on their biographies, researchers compared the figures' symptoms with those now associated with PTSD. The findings were published in *Military Medicine* in 2008.

In 1854, when Florence Nightingale was in her mid-thirties, the British subject traveled to Turkey during the Crimean War. The conflict between Russia and an alliance of France, the British Empire, the Ottoman Empire, and Sardinia, the second-largest island in the Mediterranean Sea, concerned the rights of Christians in the Holy Land.

Nightingale's mission was to care for British soldiers who suffered such ailments as frostbite, gangrene, and dysentery. The soldiers' beds were placed just 18 inches (45 centimeters) apart in an area 4 miles (6 kilometers) long. During her first winter, she often worked 20 hours per day and witnessed the deaths of more than three thousand men. Despite contracting a near-fatal illness herself, she remained in Turkey. She continued to nurse soldiers for nearly two years and stayed until the last man left for England. When she returned home, she experienced such symptoms of PTSD as fatigue, insomnia, irritability, depression, and rapid heartbeat for nearly thirty years.

When Emily Dickinson was in her teens, she was a self-proclaimed free spirit. At age thirteen, her second cousin and close friend Sophia Holland, also age thirteen, died from typhus. Emily was reportedly traumatized and became melancholy, or sad. Three more people she knew died within two years. Soon after, Emily became preoccupied by death and secluded herself. She stayed in her bedroom and refused to come downstairs to meet friends. She stopped going to church. Researchers believe this series of losses of close friends and family caused her PTSD-like isolation.

Types of Trauma

Many factors influence whether someone has the disorder. Along with physical changes in the brain, these factors include the severity and type of trauma and how long it lasted. Trauma can be explained according to the type of stressors involved.

Type 1 stressors are unexpected intense single events that last a few minutes to several hours. Terrorist

Even a camping trip can produce reminders of trauma if it exposes someone to a sight, smell, sound, touch, or taste that brings back bad memories.

attacks, rape, violent crimes, and natural disasters, such as floods, tornadoes, hurricanes, and earthquakes fall into this category.

Type 2 stressors last for a longer time period, or recur periodically. Living in a war zone or being

One awful yet all too common behavior among some sufferers of PTSD is the tendency to lash out physically. Usually, violence is directed at a partner or family members.

kidnapped or held hostage for hours, days, or longer are examples. So are such events as repeated child or spousal abuse.

Type 3 stressors are combinations of stressful events that occur over time, even if each one is less severe than those in the type 1 and 2 categories. Or it could be a combination of a major event and several more minor occurrences. For example, a tornado victim may experience additional tension when trying to get help or find a new place to live.

Contributing Factors

The likelihood of developing PTSD depends on the event itself, but also the person's experience of and reaction to the event. Those who were directly exposed to the situation or suffered a severe injury are more likely than others to be affected. The chances also depend on how serious the trauma was and how long it lasted.

A person's feelings and reactions during and after also play a role. Feeling in danger—or that a family member was in danger—increases the possibility of developing PTSD. So does feeling helpless to protect or defend oneself or others. Another indicator is the person's reaction during the event, including crying, shaking, vomiting, or feeling separated from the environment.

Extent of Damages

The characteristics of the trauma a person experienced influence the degree of negative effects. If your parent's situation involved one or more of these factors, he or she likely had a higher chance of developing PTSD:

- Did the person narrowly escape death or serious injury?

- Did the person survive an event in which a family member or close friend died?

- Was the person alone?
- Did the person have to evacuate an area or change residence afterward?

- Were there multiple deaths or injuries?

- Was the location of the event somewhere the person had previously felt safe?

- How many stressors were involved?

- How widespread or destructive was the event?

Past experiences, such as previous trauma, especially if it was unexpected, or recent life stresses, like divorce, job loss, or home foreclosure, are also factors. Substance abuse and mental health issues such as depression or anxiety also increase one's chances.

Something's Wrong

The powerful emotional and physical issues now associated with the effects of trauma were first recognized by doctors during the American Civil War. While treating wounded soldiers and others who had such illnesses as malaria, dysentery, and typhoid, doctors noticed unusually fast heart rates and irregular heartbeats.

Some attributed the condition to fatigue and called it cardiac muscular exhaustion. It became known as irritable heart syndrome, or "soldier's heart." In addition, some of these soldiers complained of nightmares and trouble sleeping. After the war, doctors found the same symptoms in civilians who had suffered emotional shock. Treatment consisted of prescribed rest and heart medications.

During and after World War I some soldiers who experienced trauma (both physical and mental) involving heavy artillery were said to have suffered "shell shock." Some thought shell shock was caused by vibrations from explosions, which were known to cause concussions or traumatic brain injury. Symptoms of these physical disorders were similar to those of what is now called PTSD. After the war the terms "combat fatigue" and "war neurosis" were used to describe the condition.

During World War II, US Army General George S. Patton reportedly ordered army hospital staff not to treat soldiers with combat fatigue, which he considered simply cowardice. The stigma remained for decades. When Nazi concentration camps were liberated at the end of World War II, mental health professionals noticed that Holocaust survivors displayed the same symptoms seen in combat veterans. They called this concentration camp syndrome.

Recent descriptions of PTSD stem from the 1970s, based partly on news stories about mental health issues, substance abuse, violence, and suicides among Vietnam War veterans. In 1980 after much research concerning the issue, a diagnosis of PTSD was added to the American Psychiatric Association's *Diagnostic and Statistical Manual of Mental Disorders (DSM)*, the standard classification of mental disorders used by mental health professionals in the United States. Today, the diagnosis applies to anyone who has experienced extreme trauma any time, anywhere, even if unrelated to war.

Support groups, both formal ones in clinical settings, and informal ones that people organize on their own, can be a great help to those suffering PTSD, especially veterans.

Teen and adolescent readers may have members of their families, including parents, who have seen combat or combat-related stress in the course of their deployments in Afghanistan, Iraq, and other war zones. Survivors of the 9/11 terrorist attacks also have suffered from PTSD. Naturally, violent crimes against women, domestic abuse, harrowing accidents, and other trauma, occur daily everywhere.

Cultural Influences

Cultural differences affect how a person evaluates an event and interprets symptoms. Even though members of other populations do react to trauma, their experiences may be quite different from symptoms of Americans. Evidence exists that the criteria for diagnosis defined for Americans may not apply in other cultures.

A study of twenty 62-year-old female Salvadoran refugees who had been exposed to a traumatic event found that all but one suffered aftereffects. In the 1999 study *Culture, Emotion, and PTSD* by J. H. Jenkins, the women denied feeling emotionally numb or avoiding situations that reminded them of the event. Instead, they reported physical symptoms of nerves and feeling feverish. Even though they suffered the symptoms as a result of trauma, they did not meet American criteria for a PTSD diagnosis.

Thanks to these and other studies, PTSD treatments can now be adapted to incorporate the trauma survivor's beliefs and customs. Principles of mindfulness and the practice of meditation, for example, have proved effective for those who practice Buddhism, as well as other non-Western disciplines.

In some cultures, patients benefit from airing and working through their experience. However in others, talking about intimate topics with someone outside the family is considered taboo. Some cultures have their own ways of coping with trauma. In Mozambique and Ethiopia, for example, those dealing with an ordeal practice active forgetting. They don't need to discuss their experience with others.

The Warrior's Return

Ancient stories form and reinforce cultural attitudes, including those of warriors returning home from battle. Homer's *Iliad* and *Odyssey*, for example,

The initial joy of having someone return home from overseas can be great. It can also be short-lived for some families when PTSD symptoms start to manifest.

include descriptions of post-stress emotions that echo symptoms defined in a modern PTSD diagnosis. The *Iliad* and *Odyssey* are epic poems thought to have been written near the end of the eighth century BCE. The *Iliad* tells the story of the Trojan War between the kingdoms of Troy (now in western Turkey) and Mycenae in ancient Greece during the Bronze Age, about 400 years earlier. The *Odyssey* covers the aftermath of the war and the Greek hero Odysseus's return home.

Stories in other cultures concern warriors who return home with feelings of rage, anxiety, sadness, and despair that force them into isolation. Other stories concern warriors who heal. These survivors get help from someone who uses nurturing, compassion, and creativity to inspire them to build relationships and gather the courage to feel emotions, rather than trying to block them. This helper represents the feminine side of each individual, whether male or female.

Examples of such stories are found in Navajo, Celtic, Greek, Mongolian, and Chinese cultures, to name a few. One Navajo story concerns twin brothers who embark on a journey to find their father, the sun. They find him, and he gives them weapons and teaches them to fight. On the way home, they bravely fight monsters and enemies that threaten the tribe. When they return, they display anger, rage, and panic. The tribe fears them and exiles them to the wilderness. Sky Mother finds them there and teaches them to sing about their suffering. The brothers return home and sing about their ordeals. The tribe learns about the brothers' experiences and welcomes them back.

The theme of a feminine character helping a returning fighter is known as the archetype of the warriors' return. An archetype is a recurrent character, action, or event that appears in art, folklore, or literature and represents universal, cross-cultural aspects of human nature. In other words, the archetype of the warriors' return illustrates that symptoms today associated with PTSD have been with humans since ancient times.

Noticing PTSD in Your Family

Much as different cultures can vary in their approach to confessing their feelings and experiences, particular families and even individual family members will approach such issues in different ways. Someone's father may be very expressive and open about hurtful events and trauma from his past. Meanwhile, the person's mother may actually be the strong and silent type. As such, they may defy the misguided stereotypes of how parents behave—that is, that fathers are emotionally distant, while mothers more emotionally expressive.

However, even among the many different kinds of households you may find in any given community there can be great variations in how a parent or guardian may or may not reveal PTSD symptoms.

Someone suffering PTSD may exhibit symptoms openly if they are alone, but may attempt to hide them from family members, especially if they have been raised to keep troubles bottled up.

Many combat veterans, especially if they have been raised in military or law enforcement families, can come from backgrounds where a stiff upper lip is encouraged, especially for males. In other families and communities, this may be true for all family members.

It may thus be harder for some children to identify or even notice that a problem has occurred. Between school and other activities, such as work, after-school teams or clubs, as well as in-person and online socializing, children may have varying degrees of contact with their parents. Still, it may not take much to see the problem: a loved one in pain.

10 Great Questions to Ask a Therapist

1. What are the chances that I will develop PTSD if I experience trauma of my own?

2. Even though my parent is the one with PTSD, will medication help me cope with my family situation?

3. How can I get my parent to tell me about the ordeal he or she went through?

4. My parent with PTSD is already going to therapy. Why do I have to go to family therapy?

5. Are there different types of PTSD?

6. Can you prevent PTSD?

7. When is the reaction to trauma normal, and when is it a disorder?

8. Can PTSD go away by itself?

9. Why do some people get PTSD and others involved in the same event don't?

10. What do I tell my friends about my parent with PTSD?

CHAPTER THREE

Family Matters

If your mother or father has PTSD, you already know that the disorder can affect the whole family. One noticeable result may be a type of ambiguous loss associated with the condition. Ambiguous loss is grief that results from a person being physically present but psychologically absent. In some ways the person you knew is gone, and you experience many of the same emotions associated with a loved one's death. Interestingly, family members of patients with Alzheimer's disease often experience the same ambiguous loss, because the personality of the person they knew has drastically changed.

A Parent's Trauma

Even though the traumatic event happened to your parent (not you), you may feel your own

A parent who seems distant, distracted, or withdrawn can be difficult to deal with. It can be a lonely experience for both the parent and the child.

set of emotions from reacting to your parent's symptoms. At times you might feel angry, scared, guilty, lonely, embarrassed, sad, worried, or hurt. Be assured that you had nothing to do with your parent's experience and response to trauma, and your own feelings are perfectly normal reactions to the situations you find yourself in.

For instance, you might feel sad or annoyed by the changes you see in your parent. You may wish he or she would return to the person you knew before the event. If you perform some or all of the care-giving for a parent who seems to have given up, you might feel overwhelmed. Even fixing a sandwich for your parent's lunch can make you feel angry at the role reversal between you and the person who is supposed to take care of you.

Another way a parent's PTSD can manifest itself is through memories and daydreams. These memories produce such emotions as grief, guilt, fear, or anger. You might notice him or her staring off into space during these times. Sometimes the brain plays tricks on PTSD sufferers, and the memories are so strong, your parent thinks the event is happening again. Seeing your parent in this state can be scary. On a general level, it's likely you'll worry about your mother's or father's overall health and whether you and your family can take good care of him or her.

Your parent's angry outbursts may scare you. They may even make you angry. So might seeing your parent have a panic attack. If that happens, try not to worry. A panic attack is not life threatening. It should last just a few minutes, and your parent will be okay again. If you are an only child or the eldest of two or more siblings and your parent's spouse is not around, it may be up to you to try to calm your parent down or at least watch over him or her in some fashion. This can be tricky. It is important to get advice from another adult on how to handle such a situation. Even though it is rare and there is little chance of such a thing occurring, some PTSD sufferers inadvertently react to stress and panic attacks with violence or violent behavior.

Staying Home

If your parent has symptoms of avoidance or numbing, he or she may stay home from places and activities that are important to you. Feeling numb to emotions

One potential type of fallout that can occur between parents and children is arguing and ending up giving each other the silent treatment.

is common among trauma survivors, causing them to withdraw from important relationships. Other PTSD effects include difficulty communicating and expressing affection.

Sleep disturbances may contribute to your parent's irritability and feeling of being too tired to do anything. This can keep him or her from joining you in activities you used to enjoy together. The more your parent feels disconnected from loved ones, the more he or she withdraws. If your parent has these symptoms, you may think your parent no longer loves you or cares about you. PTSD does not change your parent's love for you, even though it can affect his or her ability to show it.

A person with PTSD often has anxiety and seems worried about his or her own safety, even at home. That worry can extend to you and other family members. Your parent may become overprotective toward you and seem to smother you. In time, you may pick up on the fear and become worried about your own safety. Along the same lines,

One common manifestation of PTSD is a feeling of anxiety or paranoia. You may catch a parent constantly looking out the window, or checking the door to make sure it is locked.

your parent might be easily startled, causing you to tiptoe around him or her in an effort to avoid provoking irritability or anger. If your parent never seems happy about anything, you may think the negativity is your fault. The pessimism can transfer to you and negatively influence your view of the world and your future in it.

Other Effects on Children

Extensive research on the families of Vietnam War veterans has shown some adverse effects in the children of those who suffered trauma while deployed. Their parents reported that the children seemed more depressed, anxious, aggressive, hyperactive, and even showed more delinquent behaviors than children of military veterans without PTSD.

Younger children of PTSD parents often threw temper tantrums or acted out in other forms of antisocial behavior. They had more trouble getting good grades and struggled with making and keeping friends. Teens with PTSD parents had some of the same results. They had high levels of depression and anxiety, accompanied with low scores on creativity. Bad attitudes toward school sometimes resulted in truancy. Children often developed negative attitudes toward the parent with PTSD. Altogether, older siblings seemed more resilient than younger ones. Their social and personality skills did not seem affected.

Children of all ages try to avoid triggers that can set off their parent, somehow taking responsibility for the parent's irritability and low tolerance for frustration. When the parent reacts to a trigger, the child may think the parent is hostile or doesn't love him or her. And, just as the parent tries to avoid stressful events, the child may come to avoid the parent.

Some children take on the role of a rescuer. They try to fill in for the parent with PTSD and may act mature for their age. Others check out emotionally, which translates to such negative effects as fear, depression, anxiety, trouble at school, and trouble forming meaningful relationships at the time and in the future.

Troubled Couples

A parent's symptoms affect children, but they may also affect his or her spouse or partner. Disagreements and fights can be troubling. In extreme cases, these could even result in violence or at least make kids fear that separation or divorce may be on the horizon.

Some trauma survivors have trouble finding or keeping jobs. Their spouses find responsibility for money issues dumped on their shoulders, where once the trauma survivor managed or shared them. Financial strain affects everyone. You may have to give up some activities, new clothes, or other items because of a tighter family budget.

In families where a trauma survivor needs treatment, including therapy, the other parent can end up feeling burned out. The spouse without PTSD often takes on all or more of such household tasks as paying bills, cleaning, laundry, and other tasks. They also take on more responsibilities for childcare and dealing with the extended family. Many report trying to lessen triggers of PTSD symptoms.

The trauma survivor's sleep disturbances often interfere with his or her partner's sleep. Shouting out during nightmares or jerky, twitching movements during sleep often wake the partner—perhaps several times a night. Deprived of restful sleep, the spouse feels tired the next day and feels grouchy or angry. Some of the anger likely falls on you, even when you've done nothing wrong. He or she may yell at you or withdraw from you. Again, you might feel like you in some way caused the anger. Try to understand that none of these reactions is your fault, even though it may seem like you sometimes get the brunt of the anger. Make sure to talk it out with your parent and be patient, while also explaining to them their anger is sometimes misdirected.

According to the National Center for PTSD, the National Vietnam Veterans Readjustment Study found that spouses of Vietnam veterans with the disorder felt unhappy, discouraged, and had a general lack of satisfaction in their lives. About 50 percent said they

Keeping track of bills and other household responsibilities alone can be stressful for the partner who is charged with keeping it all together while the other one hopefully gets the care they need.

felt like they were on the verge of a nervous breakdown. Some reported physical and emotional violence. They also reported stress because their own needs were not being met.

All in the Family

Family members who live with someone with PTSD struggle with stress over a long period of time. The symptoms they exhibit mimic those seen in the PTSD patient and may be warning signs that family members need therapy or other intervention. Children and spouses often report the following:

Trouble falling or staying asleep

Low energy

Loss of interest in activities they used to enjoy

Lack of motivation to complete such basic tasks as schoolwork or housework

Trouble concentrating

Changes in eating habits or eating disorders

Sadness

Irritability

Excessive worry

Restlessness

Increase in physical aches and pains

Dwelling on thoughts of death

Marital Strife

The National Center for PTSD reviewed research and identified relationship problems and negative effects that occur when one marriage partner is a US military veteran with PTSD. Most of the research involved female spouses of male veterans with PTSD. However, the same issues arise when the veteran is female. Results of research posted in 2016 show these families commonly have problems with relationships, parenting, and family functioning.

Studies found that many veterans with PTSD withhold thoughts and emotions from their spouses. They also lack interest in physical intimacy. They have higher incidents of family violence and higher than average divorce rates. The National Vietnam Veterans Readjustment Study found that about 38 percent of all Vietnam veteran marriages failed within six months of the veteran's return from Southeast Asia. The percentage was twice as high for Vietnam veterans with PTSD. Those with PTSD were also three times more likely to divorce two or more times.

Is PTSD "Contagious"?

Since PTSD isn't the kind of disease caused by viruses or bacteria, you might think the disorder is not contagious. However, you might be surprised to learn that you can catch it from a parent or family member (in a manner of speaking). Just being around the trauma survivor may cause some of the same fears, anxiety, guilt, shame, or other emotions that your parent experiences. Psychologists call this occurrence secondary trauma or intergenerational transmission of trauma.

Unlike PTSD, secondary trauma as yet has no official designation as a psychiatric diagnosis. For instance, you might have nightmares about your parent's ordeal or be unable to focus on schoolwork because you are dwelling on your parent's PTSD. Or, you might feel more depressed or anxious than you did before your parent's trauma.

Although intergenerational transmission of trauma has been reported in children of combat veterans and Holocaust survivors, it is relatively uncommon. When it does happen, one or more factors contribute to it:

- **Silence.** Some parents with PTSD are reluctant to talk about details of the traumatic situation, fearing their child will be distressed by hearing them. However, if the family refuses to discuss the traumatic event itself or the thoughts or emotions associated with it, children will fill in the blanks with information from their own imaginations. The result may be more terrifying than what actually happened. Their reactions to the thoughts and emotions from the imagined story can produce a whole new set of PTSD symptoms.

- **Talking too much.** Graphic descriptions of the parent's actual trauma produce troubling images. The child can develop his or her own symptoms from picturing the event.

- **Identification.** In an effort to connect with the trauma survivor, the child may identify with him or her. Psychological identification is a process in which the child adopts the behavior, characteristics, or other aspects of a parent. In these cases, the child imitates the parent's symptoms.

- **Reenactment.** If a child is present when the parent is having a flashback, the child may actually play a role as an actor in the drama. PTSD symptoms can result in the child as if he or she actually participated in the real thing.

The chances of a child's developing secondary PTSD depend on how severe the parent's trauma is, how close to the present the incident occurred, and the parent's reaction to the trauma. The more these factors apply, the greater the possibility.

Symptoms Continue

Little research has been conducted on the long-term effects of secondary trauma. However, one study published in 2011 by Yula Dinshtein, Rachel Dekel, and Miki Polliack compared a group of 46 adult children of Israeli war veterans with PTSD to a control group of 46 adult children of veterans without PTSD. The study was based on direct responses from the adults themselves. Other studies of children's reaction to a parent with PTSD depended on observations by the children's parents.

Results of the Israeli study of children after they grew up showed higher levels of general distress among those whose parents had PTSD than the control group. The PTSD group also found higher levels of stress than the control group if the adults had been exposed to repeated terrorist attacks, even though none of the subjects in either group had direct involvement or injury from them.

Other studies have found that a children's ability to feel emotional closeness, trust others, and think that others understand them is impaired by exposure to a parent who exhibits the same systems. Not surprisingly, the PTSD group in the Israeli study also reported lower intimacy in their personal relationships, even after years had passed since their childhood experience. This seemed to confirm results of other studies, and it

Research has shown that secondary trauma, also known as intergenerational transmission of trauma, can occur even if the children did not experience trauma themselves.

also seemed to indicate that PTSD symptoms can be transferred to a younger generation from an older one.

Another aspect of the study examined the role of the now grown-up child's relationship with the non-PTSD parent during childhood. The adults reported a wide range in the expression of their symptoms. Those who had a positive relationship with the other parent reported less severe symptoms and higher levels of emotional intimacy with others than their counterparts without good attachment to the other parent. Adults who had a less positive connection with the other parent in childhood, or who came from families with high levels of violence and conflict, experienced more troublesome symptoms as adults.

The researchers suspected that the child-parent relationship may be grounded in nature as well as nurture. They pointed to other studies that looked at genetic factors that may predispose a child to greater sensitivity to traumatic events—and perhaps to develop PTSD reactions of their own in traumatic situations. Of course, one could also assume that the parent had the same biological disposition, inherited from his or her parents.

These and other studies highlight the importance of seeking help for all family members, not just the person who has PTSD. Identifying children who have a high risk for psychological disorders and emotional problems can result in them getting therapeutic help early. The studies also spotlight the need for support or individual therapy so the entire family can improve the ways they interact with others both within and outside the family unit.

Healing Families

Although the first priority is getting help for the person with PTSD, it is up to all family members to work together to rebuild connections and reach mutual healing.

To start, gather information about the disorder and share it with everyone, including age-appropriate explanations for children. Knowledge is power, and such organizations as the National Center for PTSD, the National Alliance on Mental Illness, the National Canadian Mental Health Association, Gift from Within, and others have posted helpful, reliable facts on their websites. You can also check with your library, local bookstores, and online booksellers for books on the topic.

Next, encourage the parent with PTSD to seek help. Time alone won't heal these wounds. In fact, untreated symptoms can worsen, or additional ones can develop. Other conditions

Individuals with PTSD often develop secondary problems, such as chronic pain, depression, anxiety, substance abuse, or obsessive compulsive disorder.

that commonly accompany PTSD include: generalized anxiety disorder, obsessive compulsive disorder (OCD), borderline personality disorder, depression, substance abuse, thoughts or attempts at suicide, chronic pain, and hypertension, among others.

A dual diagnosis can make treatment difficult. Some medications that ease symptoms of one diagnosis, like those for OCD, can make symptoms of the other worse. However, successful treatment of one usually improves the symptoms of the other.

Some trauma survivors don't want to go to therapy. Family members armed with accurate information can often persuade them by explaining their own concerns about the person's condition, as well as the effects of his or her behavior on the family members themselves.

Treating the Trauma Survivor

Experts disagree on whether PTSD can be technically cured. However, the symptoms can be successfully treated in many patients. Experts tend to agree that PTSD does not magically disappear on its own in most sufferers. Fortunately, many treatment options exist, and many organizations offer support for people who suffer from the condition. Treatments include medication, psychotherapy, self-management strategies, and the use of service animals. Many of these strategies also help family members affected with secondary trauma.

Question 21

Active duty military personnel sometimes resist seeking mental health treatment for PTSD. They worry that they'll lose their security clearances or be forced to leave the service altogether. These fears are because of Question 21 on the Standard Form 86 (SF86), Questionnaire for National Security Positions. Service members use this form to apply for confidential, secret, and top secret national security clearances they need to do their jobs. The US government uses the form to assist investigators in conducting background checks.

Question 21 asks whether the applicant has participated in counseling for an emotional or psychological reason in the past seven years. However, the form specifically instructs applicants to answer no if the counseling was related only to grief, marital or family concerns; adjustments from service in a combat zone; or being a victim of sexual assault.

Even answering yes to Question 21 for reasons other than PTSD cannot be used to deny an interim clearance while background checks are conducted.

(continued on the next page)

Some service members mistakenly fear seeking treatment for PTSD, thinking it will damage or end their military careers.

(continued from the previous page)

And privacy rights protect the applicant. Investigators must ask whether the applicant's diagnosis could harm his or her judgment, reliability, or ability to safeguard classified data. If the health care provider says no, the investigator asks no further questions.

Getting treatment for PTSD does not block issuance of security clearances. Instead, the factors that do cause refusal include criminal acts, failure to meet financial obligations, or activities benefiting a foreign nation.

Likewise, a PTSD diagnosis and treatment won't end a military career. In fact, the US Department of Defense leadership now officially considers the courage to seek help as a positive. Failure to seek treatment, on the other hand, can result in serious consequences. Untreated, symptoms can worsen or lead to more serious conditions that interfere with the service member doing his or her job. Numerous social problems and tragedies, including domestic violence, high rates of suicide, and elevated crime rates, as well as a propensity to engage in risky behavior, have all been linked to PTSD in returning veterans

Most medications used to treat symptoms of trauma-related stress fall into the categories of antidepressants, novel antipsychotics, mood stabilizers, and drugs for sleep disturbances. Antidepressants relieve symptoms of depression and related disorders. The most widely used include those sold under the brands Prozac and Zoloft. Each type works on different brain chemicals that affect mood. Sometimes patients

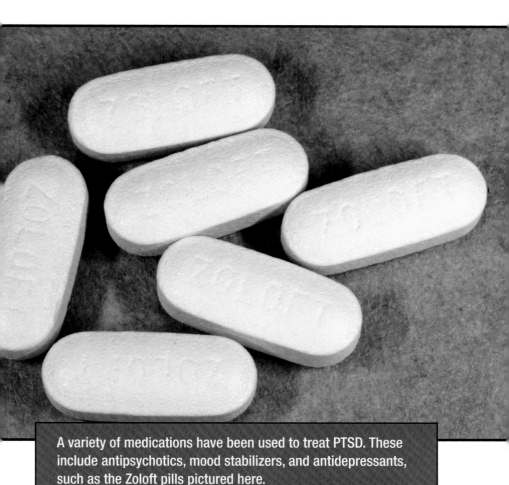

A variety of medications have been used to treat PTSD. These include antipsychotics, mood stabilizers, and antidepressants, such as the Zoloft pills pictured here.

must try several different drugs to find one that helps or one without side effects.

Novel antipsychotics are also called atypical antipsychotics. They are newly developed drugs that have a different chemical composition from earlier medications used to treat psychosis. Psychosis is a condition in which the person loses contact with reality, such as PTSD patients experiencing flashbacks. Novel antipsychotics improve the effects of antidepressants. They also ease the arising from re-experiencing trauma, emotional numbing, detachment, irritability, anger, and sleep problems.

Mood stabilizers are used to treat or prevent mood swings and mania. Mania is a mental state of excitement, euphoria, obsession, and racing thoughts. Some mood stabilizers also ease symptoms of depression. Drugs designed for sleep disorders also help trauma survivors by easing insomnia. They may also reduce anxiety. A blood pressure

Cognitive behavioral therapy helps some patients learn how their thoughts affect their feelings and actions and has been shown to help with PTSD.

drug called prazosin has also been shown to reduce nightmares.

Another drug that shows promise is osanetant, first developed to treat schizophrenia. It was found safe but ineffective for that disorder. However, research at Emory University has shown it might work to block frightening memories if taken shortly after exposure to trauma, potentially preventing PTSD.

Talk Therapy

Many PTSD patients benefit from psychotherapy. Psychotherapy is the treatment of mental or emotional issues in which patients talk about problems—commonly called talk therapy —as individuals or in groups. Older children and teens of parents with PTSD can also benefit from talk therapy. Once the trauma survivor has begun such therapy on an individual basis and shown progress in lessening symptoms, other family members

Group therapy conducted with family members or other trauma survivors can be an effective course of treatment for PTSD. Many patients find talking things out truly helps.

should participate in family therapy as a group and, if needed, get their own individual treatment.

One type of psychotherapy commonly used to treat PTSD is cognitive behavioral therapy. It explores the connection between a person's thoughts and their feelings and actions. The patient learns to turn around negative thoughts about himself or herself and the world in order to change emotions and behavior.

Prolonged exposure therapy is a type of cognitive behavioral therapy that has been widely and effectively used to treat patients with PTSD. In this technique people face their fears through gradual exposure to elements of the situation or setting where their trauma occurred, while remaining in a safe place. Patients practice controlling their fears, not just getting used to them. In many instances, symptoms decrease, and patients no longer avoid situations or sensory input that remind them of their trauma.

Spouses and Children

Spouses and children who experience secondary trauma can benefit from many of the treatments available to the person with PTSD. In addition, couples therapy is recommended for spouses or partners. Children benefit from learning about the causes of and treatment for PTSD, as well as individual therapy.

Psychotherapy for them depends on the child's age. Making sure each family member feels included in the process is important. Even children need to express their own emotions and needs.

Therapists recommend play therapy for children between the ages of three and eleven. Play therapy gives young children a way to express themselves through play and such creative activities as art, music, and drama. Children may be encouraged to act or otherwise communicate their feelings by drawing, singing, or acting them out based on what the child wants to do. Therapists interpret the results and teach the child to use a self-healing process.

A Leap of Faith

In support of people with PTSD, an organization called Warriors Ascent offers an Academy of Healing in Kansas City, Missouri, to active duty and veteran military service members, police officers, firefighters, and EMS personnel from all over the country. Warriors Ascent is a nonprofit, veteran-run organization funded by donations. It offers the academy free of charge.

The academy is a five-day program of holistic healing experiences. Holistic healing is an approach to medical care that treats the whole person, including mental, social, and spiritual factors, rather than only

Service animals can be an invaluable help to those dealing with PTSD. A nonprofit called The Wounded Warrior Project brought together this pair.

the physical symptoms of a disease. The program includes counseling, walking a labyrinth, sharing details of individual trauma, and developing trust among participants. As one graduate reported on the organization's website, "I gained twelve sisters that I trust with my heart, which is much harder than trusting someone with my life."

The most remarkable feature of the academy is its Leap of Faith. Participants climb a 40-foot-high (12-meter-high) pole wearing only a harness, then jump. The idea is to leave pain behind.

Classes of ten to fifteen divided by gender are held throughout the year. The program annually serves between 100 and 125 participants. Subjects covered include PTSD education, nutrition and basic care of the body, and social styles and group dynamics. Organizers say the program will not heal participants, but teaches them how to heal themselves.

Self-Help for Patients and Families

Some people with PTSD and their families manage their symptoms by developing their own coping techniques. However, professional mental health providers can also guide them with self-soothing strategies. For instance, distraction is one way to substitute relaxation for troubling thoughts or emotions. Some therapists

Help Is Here

Many organizations stand ready to assist you, your parent, and the rest of your family. Never hesitate to call if you need emergency help or just have a question. When using online or other digital forums, including social media platforms or chat rooms, always take steps to safeguard your privacy and safety. Beware of anonymous people who may try to take advantage of you when you are most vulnerable, especially if they advocate the use of illegal drugs or narcotics. Beware of such scams as miracle cures. Never order such products over the Internet. And watch for suspicious groups that ask for donations. If you'd like to give money, look for reputable organizations with professional-looking websites or ones whose work can be easily documented online.

Helplines:

Disaster Distress Helpline	(800) 985-5990
Gulf War Veteran's Hotline	(800) 796-9699
National Alliance on Mental Illness (NAMI)	(800) 950-NAMI [6264]
National Suicide Prevention Lifeline	(800) 273-TALK [8255]
Veteran's Affairs Caregiver Support Line	(855) 260-3274
Veteran's Affairs Coaching Into Care Program	(888) 823-7458
Veteran Crisis Line (Veterans Press 1)	(800) 273-TALK [8255]

call this method changing the channel. The patient makes a conscious choice to think about something else or take part in an activity he or she enjoys or finds interesting. Examples include taking a bath, eating a snack, watching a movie, reading a book, exercising, or calling a friend.

Another way to manage emotions is through organization. A messy environment contributes to messy feelings, including feeling out of control. Patients are encouraged to clean their homes, create a new filing system, or rearrange the clothes in their closets. These types of activities empower the patient and build confidence.

Some people simply laugh out loud to drown out disturbing thoughts or emotions. They watch funny TV shows or movies or tune in to a comedian's performance. Reading a funny book or magazine can help, too. In fact, humor is a common way people deal with distressing situations, even those unrelated to PTSD.

Additional self-management strategies include physical fitness, good nutrition, and such mindfulness techniques as meditation and yoga. Mindfulness is a mental state that involves awareness of thoughts, emotions, bodily sensations, and the environment in the present moment and without judgment. With roots in Buddhist meditation, mindfulness has resulted in physical and mental benefits and become an accepted part of treatment for stress reduction in schools, prisons, and hospitals, as well as veteran's centers.

Man's Best Friend

Service animals have been successful in helping people with PTSD cope with their symptoms. According to the Americans with Disabilities Act, a service animal is any animal that is individually trained to do work or perform tasks for the benefit of an individual with a disability, including a physical, sensory, psychiatric, intellectual, or other mental disability. Dogs are most commonly used as service animals, but one case publicized in the media in 2016 was a duck that accompanied a man with a disability on airline flights to help him stay calm. For PTSD patients, golden retrievers and Labrador retrievers are among the most popular breeds.

A service dog can remind the owner to take medication and perform daily tasks. It also provides stimulation through the sense of touch and calms an owner who gets agitated or emotionally distressed. Service animals of all kinds can help their owners with mood swings and provide a reality check for them and ground them in the here and now if they are dealing with flashbacks.

According to one study "Effectiveness of Psychiatric Service Dogs in the Treatment of Post-Traumatic Stress Disorder Among Veterans," by James Gillett and Rachel Weldrick of McMaster University in 2009, 82 percent of subjects with PTSD reported fewer symptoms after using a service dog. Another study "The Use of Psychiatric Service Dogs in the Treatment of Veterans with PTSD" by Craig Love of the US Army Medical Research and Materiel Command, Fort Detrick, Maryland, also in 2009, found 40 percent of subjects were able to reduce their use of medication after getting a service animal partner.

Other studies have found that using a service animal can, among other benefits: ease physical pain, reduce irritability and aggressiveness, lower heart rate and blood pressure, lessen symptoms of anxiety and depression, and ease feelings of loneliness.

Try, Try Again

Many treatment options exist for the trauma survivor. These treatments and strategies offer a wide range of help to someone with PTSD. Individual treatment that results in reduction of symptoms in the person who experienced the trauma benefits the family, too, simply by making life easier at home.

If one type or one therapist fails to relieve symptoms, many others are available. If he or she tried something that didn't help or visited a therapist who didn't connect, other options can be used. New interventions continue to be developed. Talking with a professional is a good way to review many options to choose from that have produced great results for others. The same advice applies to interventions for spouses and children of the person with PTSD. They can try self-management of their own symptoms or get professional help.

Moving Forward

As the child of a person with PTSD, you probably won't be able to fix the situation all by yourself. But you can do a great deal. At the very minimum, you can contribute to a healthy family environment. Helping out with chores takes some of the strain off your other parent. But the main thing you need to do is continue to work hard in school, participate in activities, and hang out with friends. Having fun is okay, even though your family is going through a rough period. However, there are some things you can do to contribute to a healthy family environment and to maintain your own coping skills and strategies.

A Supportive Presence

Family support for parents with PTSD is crucial. You can support them by realizing that their behavior does not necessarily reflect their true

Hiking or participating in other activities with a parent who is getting over PTSD can be a way to bond with them and support them in their recovery.

feelings. Someone who wants to avoid triggers that bring up upsetting memories may stay home even though he or she wants to go out with you.

You can also learn the triggers that bring on symptoms and try to minimize them. If watching the news makes your parent uncomfortable, because of frequent references to violence, conflict, and war, suggest other programming or activities that won't act as a trigger.

You can also learn ways to communicate with your parent by attending family therapy or support groups for families. A parent who is going through the challenges of PTSD needs to be surrounded by supportive people. He or she needs empathy, perhaps even more than sympathy. An empathetic way to handle the situation is something like, "I'm here for you." Other responses might be "It's so hard to experience fear of something you can't control" or "It's okay to feel that way." Acknowledge the pain and show you care about him or her.

Sometimes it's best to say nothing at all, especially if your parent starts to cry. Simply being there with a supportive presence helps the most. Don't try to make the situation go away. You can't. And there are plenty of times where, rather than recommend that your parent focus on happy things, you should instead encourage him or her to feel emotions, not bottle them up.

National PTSD Awareness Month

The US Department of Veterans Affairs' National Center for PTSD was created in 1989 to address the needs of veterans with military-related PTSD. The center's mission is to "advance the clinical care and social welfare of America's veterans through research, education, and training in the science, diagnosis, and treatment of PTSD and stress-related disorders."

As part of its mission, the center declared June PTSD Awareness Month and asked the public to help. Its website offers online promotional materials to help people learn about trauma, PTSD, and treatment options; connect with others who might have PTSD and help them find treatment; share information on social media; and plan events to raise PTSD awareness.

One way to build awareness is to wear a ribbon designed especially for military personnel with PTSD. Some ribbons for this purpose are teal. Others are black and yellow, sometimes with a red stripe or star. Black represents the unknown future for service members and their families. Yellow ribbons signify supporting troops and their waiting families until they get home. If the red stripe or star is used, it symbolizes the rage and anger symptoms of PTSD. Ribbons, jewelry, T-shirts, and other items to promote PTSD awareness are available from Etsy. Ideas for spreading the word, including tattoo designs, can be found on Pinterest.

Helping A Parent Find Help

Finding a therapist who specializes in PTSD is easy if you know where to look. You can help your parents by suggesting that they ask their family healthcare provider or member of the clergy.

Organizations also help connect families with therapists in their area. You can use your computer skills to check out websites for the Anxiety Disorder Association of America, UCompareHealthCare from About.com, and the International Society for the Study of Trauma and Dissociation. These sites have links to therapists who treat trauma. You can also search online. Just type "Find PTSD therapist in [Your City]" in your web browser.

Look online or have your parents ask about therapists' qualifications. Important factors include their professional training and experience with treating

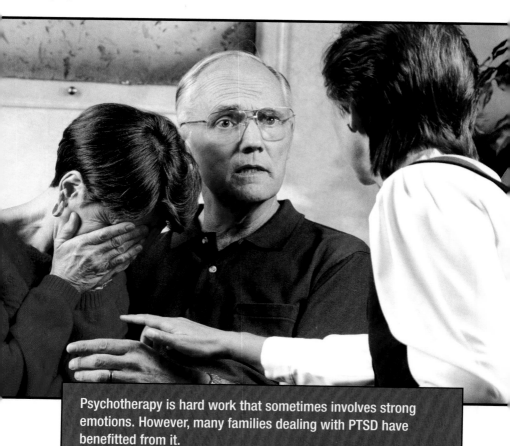

Psychotherapy is hard work that sometimes involves strong emotions. However, many families dealing with PTSD have benefitted from it.

PTSD. What is his or her approach to therapy? How are family members involved in the therapy? Does he or she also help family members?

Suicide Prevention

Another way to help your parent is to learn the warning signs that often precede suicide. According to the Department of Veterans Affairs, an alarming number of military veterans have killed themselves. A 2016 VA study found that twenty veterans committed suicide each day in 2014. The study found that 65 percent of veterans older than fifty were victims. And the rate among male veterans between the ages of eighteen and twenty-nine was more than six times higher than the national rate for the rest of the population in that age group. Suicides among first responders were also higher.

Unfortunately, many warning signs for suicide are some of the same symptoms of PTSD. You are not responsible if your parent commits this act. However, you might be able to help prevent suicide by knowing the warning signs that sometimes precede it.

If you notice any of these signs, know that you are not alone. Help is available. If you or your parent seem to be in immediate danger, call 911 in the United States or your local emergency number. If you or your parent need someone to talk to call (800) SUICIDE [784-2433] or (800) TALK [273-8255].

Bouncing Back

You can help yourself through the tough times you and your family are going through by developing resilience. Resilience is the ability to adjust to or recover from change or adversity. Ten characteristics of resilience were identified by Dennis S. Charney of the Icahn School of Medicine and Steven M. Southwick of the Yale School of Medicine. The doctors had 20 years of experience treating and studying patients who had PTSD. In their opinions, people with resilience can:

- Keep an optimistic but also realistic attitude
- Stand up to their own fears
- Rely on their own moral values
- Find comfort in religion or spiritual activities
- Find and use social support
- Learn from strong role models
- Stay physically fit
- Stay mentally alert
- Find a way to be flexible in situations they cannot change
- Seek meaning and opportunity after tragedy

These traits may be difficult to develop, but practice them as best you can. They'll help you cope with your parent's PTSD and prevent you from developing symptoms of your own.

Assert Yourself

Another trait to develop is assertiveness. Being assertive helps you get your own needs met while respecting your own as well as other people's rights. Assertiveness

Suicide Warning Signs

According to Suicide.org, about 75 percent of those who kill themselves exhibit one or more warning signs before they take their lives. These may include:

- Talking about being a burden to others, killing himself or herself, or telling family and friends goodbye

(continued on the next page)

If you or your parent are experiencing suicidal thoughts, despair, or hopelessness, it is important to reach out to someone.

(continued from the previous page)

- Withdrawing from activities, family, and friends; giving away prized possessions; increased use of alcohol or other drugs; gaining access to firearms or large amounts of drugs that can be used for overdose; or having previously attempted suicide

- Moods of depression, anger, rage, irritability, and anxiety

- Feeling trapped, helpless, hopeless, or guilty

- Experiencing stressful life events

- Family history of suicide

is not aggressiveness. Assertiveness is standing up for yourself. Aggression puts you in attack mode.

To communicate assertively, be direct, honest, clear, and brief. Clearly state what is bothering you, using specific examples, then explain the effect of the other person's behavior on you. Be sure to use "I" messages. Avoid such phrases as "You make me feel" or "You have to change this behavior." Instead focus on how you feel when the person does or says something.

You have the right to ask for what you want. So learn to clearly state how you would like things to change, but stay flexible. Your parent may not be ready to go to every basketball game or band performance, for example. Offer a compromise. Perhaps he or she can attend your activities some of the time. Select one or two events that have special importance to you, like the game against your school's biggest rival or the music performance where you'll perform a solo.

The results of your assertive communication may not be what you want or expect. If the other person responds with aggression, avoid becoming aggressive yourself. If the other person counters your complaint with criticism or a complaint of his or her own, acknowledge the concern. Then restate your own. Keep the conversation on your original topic.

Help Yourself

While most of the family focus is on the trauma survivor, you need to take time out for yourself and your own needs. Set aside time every day to do something you enjoy. Give yourself permission to be less than perfect. You're in the middle of a crisis, so you're likely to experience mental and physical fatigue. It's okay to let some things slide for a while.

Feeling a bit jumpy or irritable is perfectly normal in your situation. If you find yourself getting unusually angry at small, insignificant occurrences, take a step back before lashing out at your parent or other family members. Take some deep breaths and count to ten.

Take your mind off your own troubles by joining an activity or service group that helps others, either in school or in the community. Focusing on someone outside your family can help you take a break from your own situation for a while.

Find someone to talk to. Look for someone who will listen without making judgments about how you feel. Your friends may not be able to completely understand what you're going through. If you think none of your peers fits the bill, ask a trusted teacher, school counselor, or social worker. Or talk to a member of the clergy or a youth group leader at your place of worship. You may also find someone your own age at a family support group for those dealing with PTSD.

With the right treatment, and the support you can provide, be confident that your family can once again enjoy life as you once did, and take things one day at a time.

Peer Support

In addition to online support groups, several organizations sponsor groups in their communities. These groups meet in person and are usually led by someone who has successfully managed living with the effects of trauma in the family. You'll meet others who are experiencing or have experienced situations similar to yours. Discussing your feelings and connecting with others who truly understand your situation can help you cope with the effects of your parent's trauma on you. So can hearing others' stories. These connections can help you know that others are going through the same thing and you are not alone. You might even find new friends you can ask for help if you need it. Peer support groups also give you a chance to learn new ways to look at your situation or tips for handling challenges. Over time you can build trust in the people around you.

One way to locate a peer group in your area is to enter "PTSD Support Groups in [Your City]" in your web browser. You might even narrow the search by the type of trauma your parent experienced, and look up disaster support groups or veterans' families support groups.

Most states have a national 211 referral line that connects people with important community services, including support groups. Just dial 2-1-1. You can also contact such organizations as the National Center for PTSD, the Anxiety and Depression Association of America, the Sidran Institute Help Desk, and the National Alliance on Mental Illness. Ask for a list of community support groups near you.

Peer support can be a great way to deal with the effects of your parent's PTSD. However, if you find yourself exhibiting your own symptoms of the disorder over several months, you may need therapy or other interventions as well.

Dealing with a parent's PTSD means dealing with extreme stress that affects you and the rest of the family. Recovery can take a long time, but your support and understanding contribute to the healing process. As you develop coping skills, your parent and siblings may follow suit as everyone moves together to return to a healthy, well-functioning family.

Glossary

ambiguous loss Grief caused by a loved one's being physically present but psychologically absent.

archetype A recurrent character, action, or event that appears in art and lore and represents universal, cross-cultural aspects of human nature.

cognitive behavioral therapy A type of psychotherapy that explores the connections among a person's thoughts and how they affect feelings and actions.

flashback A memory so intense that the person believes the trauma is actually occurring.

holistic healing An approach to health care that treats the whole person, including mental, social, and spiritual factors, rather than only the physical symptoms of a disease.

hyper-vigilance A state of staying tense and alert to the surrounding environment to stay aware of potential threats.

intergenerational transmission of trauma Transferring PTSD symptoms from a parent to a child.

mania A mental state of excitement, euphoria, delusions, obsessions, and racing thoughts.

novel antipsychotics Newly developed drugs with a chemical composition that differs from earlier medications for psychosis; also called atypical antipsychotics.

panic attack A period of intense fear with sudden, unexpected onset. Most often, a person having a panic attack will have chest pain and shortness of breath or other symptoms of anxiety.

prolonged exposure therapy A type of cognitive behavioral therapy that gradually exposes patients to their fears while they remain in a safe place.

psychological identification A process where the child adopts the behavior, characteristics, or other aspects of a parent.

psychosis A condition where a person loses contact with reality.

psychotherapy Treatment of mental or emotional issues where patients talk about problems, commonly called talk therapy.

Question 21 A question on US government form SF86 that asks whether the applicant for a security clearance has been treated for a mental health issue in the previous seven years.

resilience The ability to adjust to or recover from change or adversity.

secondary trauma Trauma that occurs in others simply by being around a trauma survivor, where children or spouses develop some of the same fears, anxiety, guilt, shame, or other emotions the survivor displays; sometimes called intergenerational transmission of trauma.

Standard Form 86 (SF86) The US government form used to apply for confidential, secret, and top secret national security clearances.

survivor's guilt An emotion sometimes reported by survivors of a catastrophe, in which they think they've done something wrong by coming away from the event alive or less injured than others who died or suffered more severe wounds in the same incident.

trauma An event where serious physical harm occurred or was threatened and caused intense fear, helplessness, or horror.

Anxiety Disorders Association of British Columbia (AnxietyBC)

311-409 Granville Street

Vancouver, BC V6C 1T2

Canada

(604) 620-0744

Website: https://www.anxietybc.com

AnxietyBC is a nonprofit organization that works to increase awareness of anxiety disorders by developing online, self-help, and other resources. Its educational efforts include a Facebook page, YouTube videos, and the Mindshift app, which helps youth and young adults manage anxiety.

The Dart Center for Journalism and Trauma

Columbia Journalism School

Pulitzer Hall

2950 Broadway

New York, NY 10027

(212) 854-8506

Website: http://www.dartcenter.org

The Dart Center for Journalism and Trauma educates the media about PTSD, but also provides a short online tutorial that helps anyone learn more about emotional trauma and its effects on those who observe or suffer from violence. Its website has a self-study unit on traumatic stress, as well as summaries of current research.

Gift from Within

16 Cobb Hill Road

Camden, ME 04843

(207) 236-8858

Email: JoyceB3955@aol.com

Website: http://www.giftfromwithin.org

Gift from Within is a nonprofit organization for individuals with or at risk for PTSD and their caregivers. It provides educational materials and a roster of survivors who offer peer support.

International Society for Traumatic Stress Studies (ISTSS)

One Parkview Plaza, Suite 800

Oakbrook Terrace, IL 60181

(847) 686-2234

Email: info@istss.org

Website: http://www.istss.org

ISTSS is an international professional organization that serves to encourage and exchange information about traumatic stress. It covers trauma treatment, education, research, public policy issues, and more to encourage understanding, prevention, and advocacy in the field.

National Alliance on Mental Illness (NAMI)
3803 N. Fairfax Drive, Suite 100
Arlington, VA 22203
(703) 524-7600
Website: http://www.nami.org

NAMI is a grassroots mental health organization dedicated to Americans affected by all types of mental illness. It's a leading voice on mental health issues, encouraging awareness, education, and support through hundreds of state and local affiliates.

National Canadian Mental Health Association (CMHA)
2301-180 Dundas Street West
Toronto, ON M5G 1Z8
Canada
(613) 745-7750
Email: info@cmha.ca
Website: http://www.cmha.ca

CMHA is a volunteer organization that promotes mental health and supports recovery for those with mental illness through advocacy, education, research, and service.

National Center for Victims of Crime
2000 M Street NW, Suite 480
Washington, DC 20036
(202) 467-8700
Website: http://www.victimsofcrime.org
The National Center for Victims of Crime provides victims with support, including help with PTSD. The organization works to increase victims' rights, as well as federal and state funding for victims. It also tries to influence national policy about the issue.

VA National Center for Posttraumatic Stress Disorder
US Department of Veterans Affairs
810 Vermont Avenue NW
Washington, DC 20420
(802) 296-6300
Email: ncptsd@va.gov
Website: http://www.ptsd.va.gov

The VA National Center for Posttraumatic Stress Disorder is a federal research and education agency. Its goals include advancing clinical care and social welfare for American veterans by training professionals in diagnosis and treatment of PTSD.

Websites

Because of the changing nature of Internet links, Rosen Publishing has developed an online list of websites related to the subject of this book. This site is updated regularly. Please use this link to access this list:

http://www.rosenlinks.com/COP/PTSD

For Further Reading

Alidina, Shamash. *Mindfulness For Dummies.* Hoboken, NJ: John Wiley & Sons, 2014.

Anderson, Laurie Halse. *The Impossible Knife of Memory.* New York, NY: Viking, 2014.

Bliss, Bryan. *Meet Me Here.* New York, NY: Greenwillow Books, 2016.

Buechner, Barton, et al. *Veteran and Family Reintegration: Identity, Healing, and Reconciliation.* Santa Barbara, CA: Fielding University Press, 2016.

Fay, Deirdre. *Attachment-Based Yoga & Meditation for Trauma Recovery: Simple, Safe, and Effective Practices for Therapy.* New York, NY: W. W. Norton & Company, 2016.

Palmer, Libbi. *The PTSD Workbook for Teens: Simple, Effective Skills for Healing Trauma.* Oakland, CA: Instant Help Books, 2012.

Presley, Christal. *Thirty Days with My Father.* Deerfield Beach, Florida: Health Communications, Inc., 2012.

Underdahl, S. T. *No Man's Land.* Woodbury, MN: Flux, 2012.

van der Kolk, Bessel A. *The Body Keeps the Score: Brain, Mind, and Body in the Healing of Trauma.* New York, NY: Viking, 2015.

Vitelli, Romeo. *The Everything Guide to Overcoming PTSD.* Avon, MA: Adams Media, 2014.

Bibliography

Bergland, Christopher. "The Neuroscience of Fear Responses and Post-Traumatic Stress." *Psychology Today*, January 9, 2016. https://www.psychologytoday.com/blog/the-athletes-way/201601/the-neuroscience-fear-responses-and-post-traumatic-stress.

"How Common Is PTSD?" National Center for PTSD, August 13, 2016. http://www.ptsd.va.gov/public/PTSD-overview/basics/how-common-is-ptsd.asp.

Liebert, John, and William J. Birnes. *Wounded Minds: Understanding and Solving the Growing Menace of Post-Traumatic Stress Disorder*. New York, NY: Skyhorse Publishing, 2013.

Magers, Adam. "Supporting a Warrior Who is Suffering—Holding the Space." WarriorsAscent.org, June 26, 2016. http://www.warriorsascent.org/blog/2016/6/26/supporting-a-warrior-who-is-suffering-holding-the-space.

Matsakis, Aphrodite T. *Loving Someone with PTSD*. Oakland, CA: New Harbinger Publications, 2013.

Miller, Richard C. *The iRest Program for Healing PTSD*. Oakland, CA: New Harbinger Publications, 2015.

"Post Traumatic Stress: It's a Brain Thing." PTSD Association Canada, July 15, 2015. http://www

.ptsdassociation.com/brain-thing/2015/7/15 /improved-and-new-blog-its-a-brain-thing.

"Posttraumatic Stress Disorder." NAMI, 2016. http://www.nami.org/Learn-More/Mental -Health-Conditions/Posttraumatic-Stress -Disorder.

Price, Jennifer L. "When a Child's Parent Has PTSD." Department of Veterans Affairs, February 23, 2016. http://www.ptsd.va.gov /professional/treatment/children/pro_child _parent_ptsd.asp.

"PTSD." Pawsitivity Service Dogs. Retrieved August 25, 2016. http://www.pawsitivityservicedogs .com/ptsd.

PTSD Canada. "What Is PTSD?" Retrieved August 1, 2016. http://www.ptsdassociation.com /about-ptsd/About PTSD.

Roberts, Cheryl A. *Coping with Post-Traumatic Stress Disorder: A Guide for Families*. Jefferson, NC: McFarland & Company, 2011.

Saint-Laurent, Roger, and Sharlene Bird. "Somatic Experiencing: How Trauma Can Be Overcome." *Psychology Today*, March 26, 2015. https://www .psychologytoday.com/blog/the-intelligent -divorce/201503/somatic-experiencing.

Tick, Edward. *Warrior's Return: Restoring the Soul After War*. Boulder, CO: Sounds True, 2014.

van der Kolk, Bessel A. *The Body Keeps the Score.* New York, NY: Viking, 2014.

Williams, Kayla. *Plenty of Time When We Get Home: Love and Recovery in the Aftermath of War.* New York, NY: W. W. Norton & Company, 2014.

Wlassoff, Viatcheslav. "How Does Post-Traumatic Stress Disorder Change the Brain?" *Neuroscience & Neurology,* January 24, 2015. http://brainblogger.com/2015/01/24/how-does-post-traumatic-stress-disorder-change-the-brain.

Zayfert, Claudia, and Jason C. DeViva. *When Someone You Love Suffers from Post-traumatic Stress.* New York, NY: The Guilford Press, 2011.

Index

About the Author

Mary-Lane Kamberg is an award-winning professional writer. She is the author of *Special Ops: Snipers* and thirty other nonfiction books for young readers. She was a navy wife when her husband Ken served in the US Navy during the Vietnam Era. She is coleader of the Kansas City Writers Group and belongs to the Midwest Children's Authors Guild and the Missouri Writers Guild.

Photo Credits

Cover Angela Waye/Shutterstock.com; pp. 4–5 MoMo Productions/Taxi/Getty Images; p. 9 Caiaimage/Robert Daly/OJO+/Getty Images; p. 13 DreamPictures/Blend Images/Getty Images; p. 17 Tom Merton/OJO Images/Getty Images; p. 19 MBI/Alamy Stock Photo; pp. 20–21 sudok1/iStock/Thinkstock; p. 25 Marjorie Kamys Cotera/Bob Daemmrich Photography/Alamy; p. 28 Juice Images Ltd/Juice Images/Getty Images; p. 29 Enrique Algarra/age fotostock/Getty Images; pp. 34–35 The Washington Post/Getty Images; p. 37 Tyler Stableford/Iconica/Getty Images; p. 40 Mie Ahmt/E+/Getty Images; pp. 44–45 RBFried/E+/Getty Images; p. 47 JGI/Jamie Grill/Blend Images/Getty Images; pp. 48–49 Don Bayley/E+/Getty Images; p. 53 sturti/E+/Getty Images; p. 59 Hemant Mehta/India Picture/Getty Images; p. 62 Juanmonino/E+/Getty Images; p. 65 Steve Debenport/E+/Getty Images; p. 67 Scott Camazine/Science Source/Getty Images; pp. 68–69 Zigy Kaluzny/The Image Bank/Getty Images; pp. 70–71 FatCamera/E+/Getty Images; p. 74 Richard Ellis/Alamy Stock Photo; p. 82 Peathegee Inc/Blend Images/Getty Images; p. 86 Barros & Barros/The Image Bank/Getty Images; p. 89 DGLimages/iStock/Thinkstock; pp. 92–93 Georgijevic/E+/Getty Images; cover and interior pages background © iStockphoto.com/Sergei Dubrovski.

Designer: Nicole Russo-Duca; Editor and Photo Researcher: Philip Wolny